UNLOCKING THE G.R.O.W.N. MAN WITHIN

Becoming the man you never knew

KEITH W. BABB III

HIS EYES PUBLICATIONS

Copyright © 2016 Keith W. Babb III

ISBN: 0615976883
ISBN-13: 978-0615976884

DEDICATION

This book is dedicated to every man that's cried out for help but felt voiceless, to every man that has been imprisoned and felt like there is no way out, and for every man that's been condemned and felt like they've lost sense of who they really are.

My prayer is that you realize through the pages of this book that God hears you, He sees you, and He knows who you are.

Psalm 102:19-20, NIV "The LORD looked down from his sanctuary on high, from heaven he viewed the earth, [20] to hear the groans of the prisoners and release those condemned to death."

CONTENTS

INTRODUCTION

Society has said so many negative things about men that many of us have begun to believe that what they say about us is true. It feels even more true when we become the very things that society has labeled us as, such as unemployed, absent fathers, or even addicted to drugs. Are these labels who we really are as men or are these simply distractions, disappointments, or detours in life that make us doubt or not even realize who we were created to be. We place ourselves in mental prisons when we fail to realize our potential & purpose as men. These mental prisons are caused by our failures in life, the disappointment of not living up to the standards that others have set for us or because we simply didn't realize that our lives had purpose. Yet, what do we do when it's not just a mental prison that we find ourselves in but an actual physical prison as well? Can we find purpose in prison? How can I unlock the

G.R.O.W.N. Man within when I'm physically locked away from my family, friends, and even society itself?

This book has been specifically written for men who have experienced incarceration or even those who find themselves locked up now. My hope is that even though you may feel like life has dealt you a bad hand, or that you can never find a good paying job because of your background, or even if you will never be released out of incarceration; I want you to know that there is purpose attached to your life, there is hope even in your hopeless place, and that there is a new and G.R.O.W.N. man within you that is waiting to be set free.

As of 2012, there were 2 million men incarcerated and in addition to that, there were over 6 million men under some type of criminal justice supervision, be it probation, parole, jail, or prison. Yet, I don't see that number as disappointing or negative as some may see it. I see it as millions of men with the potential to become the man they never knew, millions of men with the opportunity to realize who they were created to be, and millions of men who can radically change the world despite their physical & mental incarceration by Unlocking the G.R.O.W.N. Man within!

1

GROUNDED IN MY VALUES

Every man or every person for that matter
has their own set of personal values. The
definition of values is *a person's principles or
standards of behavior; one's judgment of what is
important in life.* Our values drive our actions
and behavior. Every decision we make is
usually always filtered through and based
upon by our values. Despite whoever we may
want to blame for our mistakes or current

situations, at the root of it and if we can be honest with ourselves; our values ultimately led us down the paths we took in life. It is plain and clear to see that everyone has values but to unlock the G.R.O.W.N. Man within, what values are we to be *Grounded In?*

I believe every man is born with a certain set of core values, yet when we don't understand where those values came from, then as men we ultimately won't know how to handle or manage those values. Genesis 1:26-30

[26] *Then God said, "Let us make mankind in our image, in our likeness, so that they may rule over the fish in the sea and the birds in the sky, over the livestock and all the wild animals, and over all the creatures that move along the ground."*

[27] *So God created mankind in his own image, in the image of God he created them; male and female he created them.*

^{28} *God blessed them and said to them, "Be fruitful and increase in number; fill the earth and subdue it. Rule over the fish in the sea and the birds in the sky and over every living creature that moves on the ground."*

^{29} *Then God said, "I give you every seed-bearing plant on the face of the whole earth and every tree that has fruit with seed in it. They will be yours for food. ^{30} And to all the beasts of the earth and all the birds in the sky and all the creatures that move along the ground—everything that has the breath of life in it—I give every green plant for food." And it was so.*

The above passage of scripture lays out in detail, God's creation of man and it also details the values that God deposited in the first man, Adam. These are the values that I believe are evident in men today. The values of a G.R.O.W.N. Man that I believe this passage of scripture reveals are Fellowship, Family, Fruitfulness, Forefather, and Follow-ship. Let's examine each value more closely and let's see if these reflect our core values as men.

FELLOWSHIP

26 Then God said, "Let us make mankind in our image, in our likeness,

God created us with "us" in mind. Even God's intention to create man was not a solo job. God created us with careful consideration from Jesus and the Holy Spirit, so if God created us in the image and likeness of Himself, Jesus Christ, and the Holy Spirit then we have to believe that just as God was in fellowship with Jesus Christ and the Holy Spirit; we too as men must value fellowship. Fellowship is defined as *a relationship marked by ready communication and mutual understanding.* All men have a desire to understand who they are and who they were created to be and through fellowship with God we realize that. That burning desire that we have for more out of life and the burning desire to have more than what this world has to offer is only found by being in fellowship with God. God created us, so then God knows everything about us and we find out who we are by being in relationship and communication (*fellowship*) with the one who created us, God. Later in this book we will discuss the importance & the true meaning of fellowship with God in greater detail but my goal here is to simply shine light on why we value fellowship and to allow us to see that the value of fellowship comes from us being created in God's image.

Our desire for fellowship is not only connected with God but it is connected with others as well. As men we value genuine fellowship with other men and others. Remember, we were created in the image of Christ as well, who came down to earth in the form of a man and while Jesus was on earth he also desired fellowship and participated in fellowship with others. The life of Jesus on earth reflected the importance of relationships with others and that's why as men we gravitate to other men. We value those relationships and we value the ability to have fun with other men, share our lives with other men, and learn from other men. The key to fellowship with others is that those relationships must be connected to the source of our fellowship.

You adulterous people, don't you know that friendship with the world means enmity against God? Therefore, anyone who chooses to be a friend of the world becomes an enemy of God. - James 4:4, NIV

Jesus couldn't fully connect or fellowship with others who were against His Father, God. Jesus was grounded in his values! Those who couldn't accept the fact that Jesus was first in relationship with God and that they must also be in relationship with God too; simply couldn't be connected with Jesus. Jesus knew that fellowship with those who weren't connected with God would not be beneficial for his life. As Men, we have to be the same way although we desire or value fellowship with others, we must remember where the source of our values come from and then we must remain connected and grounded with those that are also grounded and connected with the source, God. Fellowship is important for men, fellowship with God and fellowship with others. Unlocking the G.R.O.W.N. Man within takes remaining Grounded in the Value of *Fellowship*.

FAMILY

27 So God created mankind in his own image, in the image of God he created them; male and female he created them.

Every man wants somebody to share his life with. More than a friend, men desire and value having someone who can be their lover and friend. Our view of family has been damaged by the media, our friends, and even the lack of having a healthy family in our own lives but that still doesn't change the fact that men desire family in the form of a wife and children. We as men struggle with our value of family and we end up devaluing (*reducing or underestimating the value, worth or importance of something*) family by sleeping with as many women as we can, by having children with women that we are not married to, and then by even neglecting our duties as fathers once we have children. Our minds tell us that no woman will ever keep us tied down but our hearts cry out to be connected with a woman for life. God even realized that it was not good for a man to be alone, *Genesis 2:18* but what happens when we as men are designed to value family but we've already messed up and devalued our family? The answer is, that we must try our best to revalue family in our lives through our intentional and consistent actions.

If you have treated the mother of your child wrong in the past, you then can begin to respect her and treat her with the worth that she deserves as the mother of your child. If you've been absent from your child's life in the past, you can now step up to the plate and reestablish a relationship with your children by calling them, spending time with them, and encouraging them to be all they were created to be. We can't change our past but we can promote our future through our actions by placing the true value of family on those that we love.

Valuing family extends even beyond our wife and children; it also involves our parents, siblings, and extended family as well. Unlocking the G.R.O.W.N. Man within involves valuing family by understanding that our actions and decisions directly impact them as well. When we choose to rob or murder someone then we must accept the fact that we just caused a mother and father to lose a son, an aunt to lose a nephew and the list goes on and on (*because we either took the life of someone else or because now we get arrested and our families can't see us anymore*). We truly value our family by moving from a "me" mentality to an "us" mentality. Every decision I make impacts "us" which is my family and we have to ask ourselves did this decision place the value on my family that they deserve? Unlocking the G.R.O.W.N. Man within takes remaining Grounded in the Value of *Family*.

FRUITFULNESS

[28] *God blessed them and said to them, "Be fruitful*

Fruitfulness is more than just making money, fruitfulness is producing results in every area of your life. No man wants to lack in anything and men value being fruitful. *3 John 1:2, NASB states* [2] *Beloved, I pray that in all respects you may prosper and be in good health, just as your soul prospers.* I believe we can all agree that we as men value fruitfulness and we have a desire to prosper but it is how we go about gaining that prosperity that gets us in trouble.

We steal, cheat, lie, deceive, even kill in our attempts to prosper. We get ourselves in a world of trouble because we did some bad things just to try to prosper. Many times that desire is not a selfish one either, we want to prosper to take care of our family, we want to prosper so that our kids can look up to us, we even want to prosper so that we can help those in need but when we don't gain that prosperity in the way that God intended; it quickly runs out or we find ourselves stuck in a hole that we actually dug for ourselves and we can't get out of that hole without help from someone else. Men across this country and world sit or have sat in jail and in prison cells because they went after prosperity in the wrong way.

The tough question is, why would men be created with a desire to prosper and be fruitful in every area of our lives, yet at times it can seem so hard to obtain that prosperity? The answer rests in the one who holds the keys to our prosperity. *Psalm 24:1, NASB The earth is* the LORD'S, and–all it contains, The world, and those who dwell in it. God created it, God owns it, so that means we need to be connected to God if we want to gain whatever our heart desires. Desiring prosperity and being fruitful isn't the problem; we were created as men to prosper. Our problem is that we don't like asking for help from God, the one who has access to the prosperity that we were designed to have. Gaining prosperity is not our problem; our problem is our unwillingness to ask and allow God to provide the prosperity that He has for our lives so that we can live the fruitful lives that we desire to have. Unlocking the G.R.O.W.N. Man within takes remaining Grounded in the Value of *Fruitfulness.*

FOREFATHER

increase in number; fill the earth and subdue it.

We hear about all the great people of the world who left a long-lasting legacy, people that have impacted individuals, communities, this nation, and the world. Men like Martin Luther King Jr., President John F. Kennedy and like Billy Graham are those who fill the books we read with their powerful legacies that they left behind. We all want we leave a legacy but what type of legacy will we leave behind? Men were created to increase in number, fill the earth, and subdue it. Increase in number does not necessarily mean having as many kids as possible but it means how many lives can you influence, how many lives that you touch that want to be more like you, and how many lives will you impact that will in turn leave your imprint on this world even after you die. Men desire to leave a legacy and to be a forefather for others.

Forefather is defined as *a person who is from an earlier time and has contributed to a common tradition shared by a particular group.* All men are forefathers to something but it seems like more and more that men have left legacies that led to higher rates of drug addiction, school dropouts, teen pregnancy, crime, and absent fathers in the lives of youth. Children tend to become what they see, so ask yourself what have you been a forefather to? Has your desire to influence left a negative or positive impact on the next generations to come?

Despite the negative influence we may have had on others, there is still hope. Men must value being a forefather, one that makes a positive impact in the life of another. Even if we've made mistakes in life, we can still teach responsibility to others by accepting our consequences, we can still teach humility to others by not blaming someone else for our circumstances, and we can still teach others maturity by not constantly making the same mistakes. Even when we find ourselves in the worst conditions such as unemployed or even in prison, we as men can still have a positive influence on others. We were created be forefathers and leave a legacy but it is up to us about what type of legacy we will leave. Unlocking the G.R.O.W.N. Man within takes remaining Grounded in the Value of being a *Forefather*.

FOLLOWSHIP

Rule over the fish in the sea and the birds in the sky and over every living creature that moves on the ground."

Have you heard the saying too many chiefs and not enough Indians, well I say too many Indians and not enough chiefs. Men must be and were created to be leaders. Every man has an area in their life that they were designed to lead, be it with their families, their children, on their jobs, or even with their friends. Men have been created to lead and with any form of leadership there comes follow-ship. When men lead, someone will always follow, yet many times we have abused our ability to gain follow-ship from others. We use our leadership to manipulate others to do things that aren't right, we lead others down the wrong path, and we destroy others to gain more leadership. God has already given each of us rule and dominion over a specific area in our life and it is our job to identify that area and simply lead well so others will follow well. Unlocking the G.R.O.W.N. Man within takes remaining Grounded in the Value of *Follow-ship.*

We must be <u>*Grounded in Our Values*</u> in order to unlock the G.R.O.W.N. Man within and I believe every man was created with a certain set of core values that are intended to shape us into the G.R.O.W.N. man that we were created to be. G.R.O.W.N. Men must value *Fellowship, Family, Fruitfulness, Forefather, & Follow-ship* but what remains the same in all of those values, is that God must be present or in other words with us to make sure that we remain grounded in those values in the right way. Our inner desires as men tell us that we need fellowship, family, fruitfulness, forefather, and follow-ship, but God is the only one who can truly fulfill those desires that we struggle with. *Psalm 37:4, NASB Delight yourself in the LORD; And He will give you the desires of your heart.* Our connection with God will not only allow us to fulfill those things that we value as men but our connection with God will allow us to remain grounded in the things that will cause us to unlock the G.R.O.W.N. Man within.

The G.R.O.W.N. Man's Prayer:

God I have placed value on a lot of things in my life that I realized aren't worth anything. I've done more harm to myself and others by chasing after desires that I didn't allow you to place in my life. Father, I ask you to open up my eyes and cause me to realize those things that you created me to value: Fellowship, Family, Fruitfulness, Forefather, & Follow-ship. Lord, not only cause me to realize them but cause me to fulfill them through you. Lord you placed them in my heart so I should be seeking you on how to fulfill those values in my life. God, help me unlock the G.R.O.W.N. Man Within by causing me to remain grounded in my values. Amen.

Psalm 16:8- "I keep my eyes always on the LORD. With him at my right hand, I will not be shaken"

2

REDEFINED BY MY INSIDE

Trends come and go, new model cars are released yearly, and no matter how new you buy something; it becomes old as soon as you walk out of the store. Items lose value, so why do we constantly try to keep pace with others by going after the next "new" or "hot" thing, such as clothes, cars, jewelry, and the list goes on and on. I believe we've placed too much value on those exterior things because we believe that exterior things define who we are as men. Not only do we believe those exterior and material things define us as men, but it seems like everyone in and outside our circle of influence believes those things define us as men as well. Media promotes only the successful man, women say they will only be with the wealthiest and best dressed man, and other men will only respect the man with most expensive and latest everything. We find ourselves in a "can't" win situation because we are constantly chasing after things that are really unable to define who were created to be.

Ecclesiastes 1:3, NKJV What profit has a man from all his labor In which he toils under the sun? Why do we chase after things and try to prove our worth with things that will eventual get old, lose its value, and ultimately be thrown away? We go through cycle after cycle of obtaining things that we hope will validate us as men and when we fail to keep up with the crazy pace of having the latest and newest, in our minds we believe that we've lost our value as men. Is always having the newest and latest even truly realistic? I'm here to tell that it's not realistic, not even for the wealthiest man in the world; even he can't keep up with the pace.

I'm not saying that material things are not worth going after, like degrees, well-paying jobs, and nice homes but what I am saying is don't let those same material things try to define you because they never will. There will always be another person who is more educated, another person who has more money, and another person that lives in a bigger home or drives a nicer car. The real question to be asked is; if what I have or own doesn't define me then what really defines who we are as men and not only what defines us but also what will not lose its value? *Proverbs 27:21b And a man is valued by what others say of him.*

What do others say about you? What type of reputation do you have? As men we are truly defined by our character. One definition of character that I found is *the actions you take to carry out the values you believe in.* Remember the values we learned that we must be grounded in to Unlock the G.R.O.W.N. Man within: Fellowship, Family, Fruitfulness, Forefather, and Follow-ship. Do your actions carry out these values? Saying we value something is one thing but defining ourselves through our character takes another level of commitment. Colossians 3:9-14 clearly defines the inside of a G.R.O.W.N. Man:

9 Do not lie to one another, since you have put off the old man with his deeds, 10 and have put on the new man who is renewed in knowledge according to the image of Him who created him, 11 where there is neither Greek nor Jew, circumcised nor uncircumcised, barbarian, Scythian, slave nor free, but Christ is all and in all.

Character of the New Man

12 Therefore, as the elect of God, holy and beloved, put on tender mercies, kindness, humility, meekness, longsuffering; 13 bearing with one another, and forgiving one another, if anyone has a complaint against another; even as Christ forgave you, so you also must do. [14] But above all these things put on love, which is the bond of perfection.

Colossians 3:9-14 also begins to reveal the man that we never knew. The man that is simply hidden beneath everything that we thought a man should be. Let's look at how we should be redefined by our insides.

COMPASSION

tender mercies, kindness,

When was the last time you felt concerned when you saw someone else suffer? We've been taught as men to embrace our toughness and to never show emotion unless it is anger, but anger can't be the only emotion we express because anger alone with no other emotional expression, will ultimately eat us up inside. I know you probably know someone who always walks around angry, just angry at the world. What does his anger accomplish;

nothing! *James 1:20, NASB for the anger of man does not achieve the righteousness of God.* We were born to care for one another and feel pain when see someone else hurt; we were designed to be compassionate. We are not just supposed to have compassion for our children, family and friends but we are supposed to have compassion for any and all who are wrongly hurt. Remember, God created "us" with "us" in mind and we must have others in mind when it comes to showing compassion. Just as James 1:20 states we can't accomplish what God has created for us as men to do, without having compassion for others. We are all connected, family or not because we were all created by the same God, so we must show compassion to all that God has created. Unlocking the G.R.O.W.N. Man within takes being redefined by our inside with the character trait of *Compassion.*

HUMILITY

humility, meekness,

If everyone reading this book can be honest with themselves then we all can say that pride has gotten us in trouble before. When we thought nobody was bigger, bolder, or better than us; we suddenly experienced that day where we found ourselves knocked off our pedestal and we realized we were wrong! Before we knew it, pride eventually caught up with us and we realized we're not as tough as we thought we were. *Proverbs 16:18, MSG First pride, then the crash—the bigger the ego, the harder the fall.* We all remember the individual falls that we've experienced in life because of our big egos. The prescription for pride is humility because the good thing about being humble is that it keeps us at such a low place that falling isn't possible.

Being humble is a place where we can recognize the gifts and talents of others, including our own and then be able to not only accept the gifts and talents of others but celebrate them too. People have killed people over pride and jealousy but humility keeps us out of those situations. Pride can lead to someone dying but humility causes us to die to ourselves by killing our egos.

I've heard one definition of humility as *having strength under control,* so it's not that we are weak as men when we are humble, but humility actually reveals our strength. It takes strength to walk away from a hostile situation, it takes strength to keep our opinions to ourselves for the sake of someone else, and it takes strength to define a man by his willingness to walk in humility. Unlocking the G.R.O.W.N. Man within takes being redefined by our inside with the character trait of *Humility*

GRACE

*longsuffering; [13] bearing with one another, and
forgiving one another*

What would you do if someone lied to you
multiple times, what would you do if you had
a friend that always had negative things to say
about you, and what would you do if a close
sibling repeatedly stole money from you?
Many of you would say that you would stop
talking to that person, or that you would cut
them off because that person isn't a real friend
anyway, or maybe even that you would lie or
steal from them since they did the same thing
to you, but the G.R.O.W.N. Man within has to
be full of grace! Grace is undeserved favor, so
even when others don't deserve it we are
supposed to extend them not only a second
chance but numerous chances. That's what we
desire, someone to extend us another chance
and as G.R.O.W.N. Men we are obligated to
do the same for somebody else.

We've made mistakes in our lives that have slowed down or even stopped us from making progress and moving forward in life. We've made mistakes that have caused us to ruin relationships with our children and families. We've made mistakes that have made it more difficult to find a job. We've even made mistakes that have affected the rest of our lives, yet if we could make it happen, we would want someone to give us another chance to correct our mistakes. Even when we don't believe ourselves to deserve it, if the opportunity was offered to us then we would take that chance to get it right and that chance is only extended through grace.

Grace is more than just giving someone another chance, but grace also involves forgiving them for what they did wrong. Grace involves forgiving and not holding it against them. We can't forgive someone but continue to bring up whatever that person did wrong, again and again. Grace involves giving others a clean slate. Grace means I don't hold your past against you and I allow you to start over brand new. True grace is something I believe we all desire because no one is perfect and at some point in our lives we all will need grace. G.R.O.W.N. Men understand the need for grace and the importance of giving grace to others.

Just as we desire grace, our lives should be full of grace. When people treat us wrong, we should extend them grace. When people mistreat us, we should extend them grace. When people talk about us behind our backs, we should extend them grace. Grace impacts and influences the other person more so than us. Grace is so influential that it causes the lives of others to change. As men, not only do we define ourselves by the amount of grace we extend to others but we literally redefine and reshape the lives of others because our acts of grace are so impactful in the lives of others. Think of how someone who lied on you would feel if they realize that you gave them another chance in your life despite what they did to you. They would be moved by grace to never do that to anyone again let alone you! Unlocking the G.R.O.W.N. Man within takes being redefined by our inside with the character trait of *Grace*.

LOVE

[14] But above all these things put on love

Love can be such a tricky word to define. We all want it but few know what love really means or what real love even looks like. Even the dictionary has different meanings for the word love: *a profoundly tender, passionate affection for another person. 2. a feeling of warm personal attachment or deep affection, as for a parent, child, or friend.* I believe even the dictionary's definition of love falls short of what it truly means. I think we have already captured the true essence of love in this chapter which is compassion, humility and grace. Without those qualities, I think it is impossible to love. Love must show great concern for others just as with compassion, love must put others before ourselves just as with humility, and love must always extend others with another chance even when they don't deserve it just as with grace.

Colossians 3:14 calls love the bond of perfection. Think about it in this way, love that consists of compassion, humility, and grace creates the man of perfect value. When we can be redefined by our inside by developing our character through having compassion, humility, and grace which ultimately is love; we create a man that has the type of value that will never lose its worth. Many men chase after things to give themselves value and validate them as men but it is our character that determines who we really are.

We must be _Redefined by our Inside_ in order to unlock the G.R.O.W.N. Man within because our inside which is our character is where our true value lies. Chasing anything can wear you out, especially when the things we chase after begin to lose their value and worth and then we have to chase after something else. We lose focus on ourselves when we put all our efforts into getting things such as cars, clothes, and money simply so others will accept us. Our focus becomes proving our worth to others rather than building worth within ourselves; worth that is built by shaping our character with *Compassion, Humility, Grace, which ultimately leads to Love.*

The G.R.O.W.N. Man's Prayer:

God, I have spent my entire life trying to live up to the standards of others and trying to define myself by the things that I have. Lord, I ran myself into the ground chasing after things like women, cars, money, and clothes. I have even done some things that I knew were wrong just to obtain those things that will someday lose value. Father, forgive me for thinking that those things defined me as a man and Lord thank you for allowing me to see what creates me to be a man of perfect value: Compassion, Humility, Grace, & Love. God, cause me to replace the material things that are on the outside with the things that I need on the inside to build my character. God, help me unlock the G.R.O.W.N. Man Within by causing me to be redefined by my inside. Amen.

1 Samuel 16:7b- "The LORD does not look at the things people look at. People look at the outward appearance, but the LORD looks at the heart."

3

OWNING MY ACTIONS

One of the biggest roadblocks in life that keep us from moving forward, being successful, and reaching our goals is that we blame others for where we are in life. We blame our fathers for not being in our lives, we blame the police for wrongfully arresting us, we blame the government for not providing enough jobs, and the list goes on and on. Men especially find it easier in life to simply blame someone else rather than accepting the fact that maybe we had something to do with where we are in life today. Maybe it was a decision or a choice we made that has us where we are. We waste too much time that we can't get back when we use it to blame others rather than choosing to accept the consequences of our poor choices and move forward.

Why do we choose to blame others rather than realizing our current circumstance may be because of us? I believe with every bad choice, every bad decision, and every bad circumstance; men begin to believe that those choices, decisions, and circumstances make them bad men. We can't accept those consequences because when we make a mistake, we believe that it makes us less of a man. We count it as another failure on our record and another failure as a man, but I believe that when we accept our mistakes and bad decisions it actually grows us as men.

Think of the impact you can have on your children that you may have neglected when you can own up to your mistake and begin to form a relationship with them or the impact you can have on the family whose child that you took the life of if you own up to your actions and ask for the family's forgiveness. The weight of the mistake is not only lifted from your life but it's also lifted from the life of those that your mistake affected. Your child would consider you a better father because of it and that family will consider you a better man because of your willingness to own up to your actions. When men can understand that all of us make mistakes or experience failures in life but it is those men that don't blame others but accept their mistakes and failures who are able to make forward progress and succeed in life. Yet, there is more to owning our actions than simply just accepting that we are the source or reason for our failures, let's look at 1 John 1:9, MSG

On the other hand, if we admit our sins—make a clean breast of them—he won't let us down; he'll be true to himself. He'll forgive our sins and purge us of all wrongdoing.

It's one thing to accept our mistakes but it is another thing to be given a clean slate from our mistakes. We're not always promised that we will get a clean slate from those that we may have hurt with our wrong mistakes but we are promised that God will give us a clean slate if we accept our mistakes and ask for His forgiveness. If God is willing to forgive us then we must trust the fact that God will also work on the hearts of those we may have hurt with our mistakes. Unlocking the G.R.O.W.N. Man within and becoming the man you never knew takes owning your actions through:

ACKNOWLEDGING & APOLOGIZING

On the other hand, if we admit our sins

Owning our actions involves us acknowledging & apologizing for our mistakes, wrongdoings, and failures to not only ourselves and those we hurt, but ultimately to God. We must realize that we can't blame others for our current situations no matter how much others may have played a role in those mistakes; we have to accept the role that we played and stop lying to ourselves and acknowledge that we messed up. It becomes a burden lifter when we can acknowledge & apologize for the roles we played in our failures because as much as we want to blame others, we can't control what they might do to help resolve our situations but we can control what we can do to help resolve our situations. As men we won't make progress in life if we don't first acknowledge that we've made our fair share of mistakes and failures and that the blames lies squarely on our shoulders.

Not only must we must acknowledge those wrongdoings to ourselves but we also must acknowledge & apologize to those we hurt with our wrongdoings as well. Who have you hurt with your mistakes: your children, family, friends, or others then let them know what you did was wrong, by any means necessary try to apologize for your wrongdoings towards them. *Romans 12:18, NIV If it is possible, as far as it depends on you, live at peace with everyone.* Some of you may be asking how can I acknowledge & apologize for my wrongdoings to those I hurt when those I hurt won't talk to me? You can write a letter or you can send a message through someone they know. You can't be worried about their response but you should be more concerned about how much effort you put into letting them know that you hurt them as a result of your mistake and that you apologize for allowing your wrongdoing to be the source of their pain. Even if they don't forgive you, your job is at all costs and with all your efforts exhausted to acknowledge & apologize for your wrongdoings towards them.

After we have acknowledged our wrongdoings to ourselves and to those we hurt, we then must acknowledge our wrongdoings to God. Some of you may be thinking, why do I have to acknowledge my wrongdoing or mistakes to God? Well, because God sees our wrongdoings as sin and sin then separates us from the one who is able to forgive us of our sin. Despite what those we may have hurt do with our acknowledgement & apology of our wrongdoing, it's God who is able make us brand new when we acknowledge our wrongdoings to Him. If we want to get to the place where our records are made clean then we must come clean about our mistakes, failures, and shortcomings with God. Unlocking the G.R.O.W.N. Man within takes owning our actions through *Acknowledging & Apologizing.*

ABSTAINING

make a clean breast of them

Owning our actions takes more than acknowledging & apologizing because once we acknowledge & apologize for our wrongdoings, we must also strive to abstain from future wrongdoings. It's like a child that tells their mom that they are sorry for being bad in school but continues to be bad in school day after day. Your acknowledgement & apology means nothing if you continue to make the same mistake over and over again. There are plenty of men who have owned up to their mistakes but even after they own up to them, they continue to make the same mistakes. You can't tell your child that you are sorry that you missed their birthday party and then miss next year's party as well. Your child will begin to not accept your apology or any future apologies from you either because they won't be able to trust what you say. You have to make every effort to show that your acknowledgement & apology was genuine and you do so by abstaining from making the same mistakes again. Abstain means to *hold oneself back voluntarily, especially from something regarded as improper or unhealthy.*

The word that sticks out to me in the definition of abstain is "unhealthy." Again, we all make mistakes but continuous mistakes are unhealthy; unhealthy for us, unhealthy for those that our mistakes have impacted, and unhealthy for the relationships that mean so much to us. When unhealthy things are left untreated it usually results in the death of something. When we fail to abstain from future wrongdoings, we kill our reputations and relationships. Why would we risk our reputations by continuing to make the same mistakes over and over again? Why would we risk our relationships with our children, family, and friends because we can't abstain from future wrongdoings? *1 Peter 2:11, NIV Dear friends, I urge you, as foreigners and exiles, to abstain from sinful desires, which wage war against your soul.* Relationships are necessary for men and we wage war against the very relationships that we need in our lives when we fail to abstain from future wrongdoings and mistakes. Abstaining protects our reputation and it protects our relationships that are simply not worth losing! Unlocking the G.R.O.W.N. Man within takes owning our actions through *Abstaining.*

ACCEPTING

he won't let us down; he'll be true to himself

Owning our actions takes acknowledging & apologizing for our wrongdoings, abstaining from future wrongdoings, and it also takes accepting God's forgiveness for our wrongdoings. Despite even our best efforts, we may have family, friends, and those we hurt who won't be willing to forgive us. Many of us have done things that we don't even want to forgive ourselves for. We may even believe that nobody should forgive us and that we deserve whatever we got and more for the wrong things that we've done in life, yet God wants to freely and fully forgive us.

God is actually seeking for those, He can forgive. Remember, God created us for fellowship with others and ultimately fellowship with Him. Fellowship with God isn't possible unless we allow God to forgive us for our every bad decision, choice, and action. God isn't like everyone else, He won't say that He forgives us and then bring up our past mistakes and failures and put them in our faces time and time again. Not only does God want to forgive us but He wants to wipe our record clean, *1 John 1:9c, MSG He'll forgive our sins and purge us of all wrongdoing.*

Some of us would pay a lawyer all the money we can to try to expunge our records but even expunging our records doesn't stop the fact that our records still exist. God isn't looking for you to pay anything but He is asking you to accept His forgiveness free of charge so that He can fully wipe your record clean. No longer will you have to regret the mistakes you've made in life or regret the fact that you have hurt people because God wants to freely and fully forgive you if you are willing to accept His forgiveness. God doesn't just want to expunge your record, He wants to wipe your record clean and you can allow Him to do so by accepting His forgiveness. Unlocking the G.R.O.W.N. Man within takes owning our actions through *Accepting*.

It takes <u>O</u>*wning our Actions* in order to Unlock the G.R.O.W.N. Man within but owning our actions is more than confessing what we did wrong. We have to stop blaming others for where we are in life and acknowledge to ourselves, those we hurt, and ultimately acknowledge to God that we've made mistakes along the way. We also have to abstain from future wrongdoings or we risk killing our reputation and relationships.

Finally, we must accept God's forgiveness because He and only He can forgive us to the point where our mistakes and wrongdoings will no longer be heavy on our hearts and minds. If you want to become the man you never knew, it takes you owning your actions through *Acknowledging & Apologizing, Abstaining, & Accepting.*

The G.R.O.W.N. Man's Prayer:

Father, I've spent too much of my life blaming others for where I am now. Time after time God, I was not willing to accept the fact that I was the main source of my problems. God, I recognize now that I was wrong so God I acknowledge all my wrongdoings to myself, to those I hurt, and most importantly to you. God with your help, I will abstain from future wrongdoings. God help me to not continuously hurt myself and others by making the same mistakes over and over again. I can't afford to have my reputation and my relationships die because of my unhealthy wrongdoings. Father, I ask, seek, and accept your forgiveness. I realize that your forgiveness is what I ultimately need. No matter if others don't forgive me; your forgiveness is what wipes my record clean. God, help me unlock the G.R.O.W.N. Man Within by owning my actions. Amen.

Psalm 32:5- "Then I acknowledged my sin to you and did not cover up my iniquity. I said, "I will confess my transgressions to the LORD." And you forgave the guilt of my sin."

4

WILLING TO BE SELFLESS

We live in a world where it's all about "Me." Everyone is looking out for themselves. People say things like *"I'm all I got"* or *"If I'm good then everything else is good."* I'm not saying that we shouldn't focus on personal goals and personal achievements but what would happen if we started to think like our creator. Remember God, Jesus Christ, and The Holy Spirit created "us" with "us" in mind so why can't we live life with "us" in mind. G.R.O.W.N. Men need to live life with others in mind; not just our family, children, and friends but we have to consider the one in my cell, the one I work with, and even the one that I don't know.

I believe that's why we can be so quick to hurt others, steal from others, and even kill others because others don't mean anything to us. God realized the importance of others in the life of a man, *Genesis 2:18a, NKJV And the* LORD *God said, "It is not good that man should be alone.* Why would God say that it is not good that man be alone? God knew and we know that we need each other, but our problem is sometimes we act like and live our lives like we don't need anybody. Alone, we can't accomplish all that we were created to accomplish, so why do we try to do it alone? We try to handle life and the issues of life alone because we are selfish and selfishness gets us nowhere.

Galatians 6:7, MSG Don't be misled: No one makes a fool of God. What a person plants, he will harvest. The person who plants selfishness, ignoring the needs of others—ignoring God!—harvests a crop of weeds. All he'll have to show for his life is weeds! That's why it's so easy for us as men to walk out on our kids, walk out on our responsibilities, or even rob and kill those we don't even know; because we are selfish. Selfishness causes weeds to grow in our lives and those weeds choke the life out of our attempts to have real relationships or real success in our lives. What's the benefit of living a selfless life? A life that is more than just thinking of others but a life that actually puts the needs of others before our needs. Let's look at Ecclesiastes 4:9-12, NIV:

⁹ Two are better than one,
because they have a good return for their labor:
¹⁰ If either of them falls down,
one can help the other up.
But pity anyone who falls
and has no one to help them up.
¹¹ Also, if two lie down together, they will keep
warm.
But how can one keep warm alone?
¹² Though one may be overpowered,
two can defend themselves.
A cord of three strands is not quickly broken

SUCCESS

Two are better than one, because they have a good
return for their labor

This is not to say success is not achievable to just the individual but this is to say that our success is greater when we are willing to work with one another and support one another in whatever we do. No matter what type of project you may be working on, if it's a car wash business; you may have the money to start it up but someone else may have the skills to manage the business or the knowledge to know where to get the supplies for the business at a lower price. We can go all in by ourselves but we miss out on the greater success that we could achieve if we work together with someone else.

We've all been created with unique gifts and God can use those gifts by themselves but when we use those gifts together with the gifts of someone else then the outcome is even greater. Think of a band; the drums are good by themselves but when you put the drums with a guitar and a keyboard, you get an amazing sound that a drum simply couldn't make on its own. It's the same way with you! You are good by yourself but when you can connect and use your gifts & talents with the gifts & talents of someone else, you can make an amazing combination that will produce a greater success than you could've ever achieved on your own. Unlocking the G.R.O.W.N. Man within involves us willing to be selfless which gains us the benefit of *Success*.

SUPPORT

If either of them falls down, one can help the other up.

Just as with the success that comes from being selfless; there is support when we are willing to be selfless. You can believe all you want that you don't need anybody but at some point in your life, you will need someone's support. We've needed support for a problem, we've needed support with finding a job, we've even needed support to be bonded out of jail. I will even go as far to say that we've been created to need support in some type of way in our lives. Just think about when we were born, we began life needing the support of our parents and family; we couldn't feed and raise ourselves. My prayer is that even now this book is supporting you to become the man you never knew. A man's need for support, really is a part of our DNA.

When we are selfless, it creates an open invitation to receive support. Think about areas in your life where you could use support. Is it support to deal with an addiction, is it support to learn how to cope with the loss of a loved one, or is it simply support with learning a new skill? Well, that support is available when we can put our pride down and begin to focus our attention on the lives of others. There are many people in the world waiting to support us but we are holding the key that will let them in and that key is being selfless. Unlocking the G.R.O.W.N. Man within involves us willing to be selfless which gains us the benefit of *Support*.

SECURITY

Also, if two lie down together, they will keep warm.

Security is more than just safety, but it involves having someone that you can count on and trust consistently. Think about what *Ecclesiastes 4:11a* says; lying down together to get warm. Warming up usually takes a length of time. You don't just cuddle with someone and instantly become warm, there is a process in doing that. You have to get close, hold each other, and you have to do so for a while until you begin to get warm, so we see that there is time involved. Also you don't just get close with someone you just met; it is usually someone you have a close relationship with. Close relationships are also developed over time by having opportunities to learn to trust the other person. Being selfless allows us to open ourselves up to relationships that can develop through time and trust.

Men need relationships that provide security, especially security with another man. Who can you share your deepest thoughts, hurts, and pains with? We need relationships with those we can consistently count on. That doesn't mean they will always be there but it does mean we can consistently trust their hearts and their advice for us. If we are selfless then it causes us to develop relationships with others who are selfless as well, so we can trust their hearts and advice because those who are selfless, live life with "us" in mind. Those who live life with "us" in mind don't just think about the needs of others but they actually put the needs of others before theirs. Unlocking the G.R.O.W.N. Man within involves us willing to be selfless which gains us the benefit of *Security*.

STRENGTH

Though one may be overpowered, two can defend themselves.

We all get weak sometimes. Dealing with life can make us weak; disappointing our children, losing friends to violence, losing a family member to sickness or even not getting the job that we applied for can all make us weak in life. Emotionally we can become weak and mentally we can become weak. We lose the desire to try to do the right thing and we can even lose the desire to live life. There are times in every man's life where we become weak.

The problem is not becoming weak, the problem is that when we become weak; we have no one to help strengthen us and encourage us to keep moving forward and to not give up. People who find themselves in emotionally and mentally weak places and don't have anyone to help strengthen them, are usually the ones that commit suicide. We think it is easier to take ourselves out rather than to hold on and deal with life, especially when we are weak. Selfish people die alone but selfless people have others who can help them fight against death!

This is not saying that these people in our lives take the place of God but this is saying that God will send people in your life that were created to help strengthen you with encouragement, prayer, and wisdom, *1 Thessalonians 3:2, NASB and we sent Timothy, our brother and God's fellow worker in the gospel of Christ, to strengthen and encourage you as to your faith.* We all need strength from time to time and being selfless opens the door to receiving that strength, so that God can send someone to strengthen and encourage us in our times of weakness. Unlocking the G.R.O.W.N. Man within involves us willing to be selfless which gains us the benefit of *Strength.*

Some say pride is the number one killer of men. Not guns, drugs, women, or health concerns but pride. Pride causes us to put ourselves in positions and places where we lose our lives. Many of us have seen men who thought they were better than someone else and then we saw them killed by the gun of that someone else or because men didn't want help from anybody so they thought they would solve their problem by overdosing on drugs. Pride can be a lethal killer but our willingness to be selfless can be our key to life. We will all come to a point in life where we will need someone else and being selfless opens the door for them to come in. We must be <u>Willing</u> *to be Selfless* in order to Unlock the G.R.O.W.N. Man within and a selfless life comes with the benefits of *Success, Support, Security, & Strength.*

The G.R.O.W.N. Man's Prayer:

Father, I realized that I have had a selfish mindset for a long time. All I cared about was me, myself, and I. God I didn't realize how many people I neglected and hurt because everything was all about me. Father, forgive me for having so much pride in my life and for thinking only about myself. Thank you for allowing me to see the benefits of a selfless life and Lord help me to live a selfless life. God, help me to not only to think of others but to even be able to put the needs of others before mine, because if I do I will receive the benefits that a selfless life provides: Success, Support, Security, & Strength. God, help me unlock the G.R.O.W.N. Man Within by me willing to be selfless. Amen.

Galatians 6:2- "Carry each other's burdens, and in this way you will fulfill the law of Christ."

5

NAVIGATED BY MY PURPOSE

God has given us a collective purpose as men and I hope that I revealed that to you through the first four chapters of this book. God has called men to be **G**rounded in our Values, **R**edefined by our Inside, **O**wning our Actions, & **W**illing to be Selfless. God has called all men to this collective purpose and if you recognize that if you take the first letter of each purpose that we've been called to, it spells out *GROW*. This collective purpose that God has called all men to will allow us to *grow* in maturity, yet to Unlock the G.R.O.W.N. Man within that God has called you to be, it takes more than just maturity but it takes you being navigated by your individual purpose.

No matter where life has you: unemployed, homeless, in jail or in prison; it is never too late to understand and to accept the individual purpose that God has for your life. Money, education, or even your location can't stop you from being who God created you to be; all you need to do is be obedient to what God has called you to do. When you understand your unique and individual purpose then your every decision, choice, and action will be guided by that purpose. You won't have to worry about if your life is headed in the right direction, because once you realize the right purpose for your life, it will always lead you down the right path for your future. Romans 8:30 reveals what happens when we understand and accept our individual purpose:

And those he predestined, he also called; those he called, he also justified; those he justified, he also glorified.

PRE-PLANNED - *he predestined*

God has already written the end of your story! God wrote a plan for your life before you were even born; he knew who your parents would be, where you would live, and the lives that you would impact, but with any story there are always those who want to rewrite the ending. When we are not navigated by our purpose, we rewrite the perfect story that God has already pre-planned for our lives, *Jeremiah 29:11, NASB For I know the plans I have for you," declares the* LORD, *"plans to prosper you and not to harm you, plans to give you hope and a future.* Why rewrite a perfect ending?

If you want to make sure that your life has

the ending that it was designed to have, you have to allow the author, God to finish your story. Don't get in the way of God finishing your story. Even when life seems hard, when we make mistakes, and even when others try to hurt us; when we are navigated by our purpose we can trust the fact that God's purpose for our lives is pre-planned and we can trust the fact that everything will ultimately work together for our good, *Romans 8:28, NASB And we know that God causes all things to work together for good to those who love God, to those who are called according to His purpose.* Unlocking the G.R.O.W.N. Man within takes me being navigated by my purpose which leads me to a life that God has *Pre-planned.*

PRE-SELECTED - *he also called*

You were God's first round draft pick! Not only did God pre-plan your life but he pre-selected you as well. God chose you to be His and when you belong to someone you receive all the benefits of the owner. God's love, His protection, His riches, and all that He has, belongs to us because we were pre-selected. When we are navigated by our purpose, we are then given access to all that God has for us.

Think about any first round draft pick. They receive a guaranteed contract which means they have to be paid by the team that selected them and they will remain on that team to the end of their contract. The team is obligated legally to make sure those things happen. God also offers a guaranteed contract with those who are navigated by their purpose. God will make sure that you get all the benefits that come with being on His team but the good part is that God allows you to remain on his team forever as long as you choose to be on it. God's contract doesn't run out or end, as long as we continue to be navigated by the purpose that God has given us. Unlocking the G.R.O.W.N. Man within takes us being navigated by my purpose which leads us to a life that God has *Pre-selected.*

PRE-APPROVED - *he also justified*

You have nothing to prove! God has already approved you, when you are navigated by your purpose. People will notice when you accept and walk in the special and unique purpose for your life. It may not make everybody happy and people may not truly understand but none of that matters because God has already given you all the approval you need. You will never have to live your life trying to please somebody else or wondering about how others will feel about the decisions you make because when you are navigated by your purpose all other approvals are out the window because God approved you for your purpose before anyone could even have an opinion. Unlocking the G.R.O.W.N. Man within takes me being navigated by my purpose which leads me to a life that God has *Pre-approved.*

PRE-PARED - *he also glorified*

God wants to put you on public display! God has a special place in His trophy case just for you and it has been pre-pared. God has uniquely crafted you, you are not a generic copy but you were handcrafted so that He could put His prize possession on display, *Ephesians 2:10, NASB For we are His workmanship, created in Christ Jesus for good works, which God prepared beforehand so that we would walk in them.* People have probably told you that you were never good enough, that you would never be anything, or that there is nothing special about you, but God says there is something special about you and He wants to show the world just how special you are.

There is a place of glory, of honor, and of prestige that God has pre-pared for us but it takes us being navigated by our purpose to be put in that place of glory and honor. God isn't trying to put you in this place so that you can show others you made it but God is trying to put you in this place so that others would want to be navigated by their purpose too. God wants to use your life as His personal advertisement so that He can display how He can use you and others for great and special purposes despite our circumstances. God can put you on display even if you are in jail or prison and He can use your life to change the lives of others if you allow Him to. Unlocking the G.R.O.W.N. Man within takes me being navigated by my purpose which leads me to a life that God has *Pre-pared*.

Who wouldn't want their lives to positively influence others? God can do it, if we allow Him to and if we are navigated by our purpose. We've all made mistakes that have negatively influenced the lives of others, we may even think that we've ruined the lives of others because of our mistakes but God is giving us the opportunity to put all of that behind us. If we allow Him to put us in the place that has been pre-pared for us, then He can reveal to the world the unique purpose that He has designed for our lives.

It's not enough to *grow* if we never become G.R.O.W.N. Men. God has created us to be G.R.O.W.N. Men but if we aren't navigated by our purpose, we will never become the men that we never knew. You may be wondering how can you find out the purpose for your life? The source of our purpose is found in the one who created us and we have to be connected to God if we ever want to know the individual purpose that we were created for. Accept God's purpose for your life and stop trying to fulfill your own purpose for your life. We must be <u>N</u>avigated by our Purpose to Unlock the G.R.O.W.N. Man Within and God's individual purpose for us as men causes us to have lives that are *Pre-planned, Pre-selected, Pre-approved, & Pre-pared.*

The G.R.O.W.N. Man's Prayer:

God thank you for creating me for a special and unique purpose. I can't believe that you would use my life for great things despite the mistakes that I have made. Lord, I realize that you want to use me no matter where I find myself in life. It doesn't matter how much money I have, how much education I have, or even if I am in jail or prison, God you simply want me to be navigated by the purpose that you created for my life. God, I don't want to rewrite the story for my life; I want to follow the script that you've already written. God you know the purpose for my life so help me understand and accept the individual purpose for my life, because I want a life that is Pre-planned, Pre-selected, Pre-approved, and Pre-pared. Father, help me unlock the G.R.O.W.N. Man Within by being navigated by my purpose. Amen.

2 Timothy 2:21- "Those who cleanse themselves from the latter will be instruments for special purposes, made holy, useful to the Master and prepared to do any good work

CONCLUSION

My prayer is that this is not really the conclusion but actually the beginning. The beginning for you to become the man that God has created you to be. My hope is that through the pages of this book that you realized that God has a plan for you, despite what others may say or what your current circumstances may look like. My prayer is that you now have a desire to be a G.R.O.W.N. Man, one who is <u>G</u>rounded in your Values, <u>R</u>edefined by your Inside, <u>O</u>wning your Actions, <u>W</u>illing to be Selfless, and <u>N</u>avigated by your Purpose. My hope is that you finally realized that there is man that you never knew within you that is waiting, crying, and yelling to be set free.

This book is more than just 5 simple steps to becoming a G.R.O.W.N. Man because by yourself you can't become a G.R.O.W.N. Man. Only God truly holds the keys to Unlock the G.R.O.W.N. Man within and you have to be in relationship with Him to gain access to those keys. I know some of you who have read this book may already have a relationship with God through Jesus Christ so my desire is that you continue to grow in your relationship with Him so that you can grow into the G.R.O.W.N. Man you were called to be, but for those of you who haven't experienced the love of Christ, I am begging you to accept Him in your life.

God loves you so much and desires so strongly for you to be a G.R.O.W.N. Man that He gave His only son so that Jesus could die for us so that we could have life, *John 3:16 "For God so loved the world, that He gave His—only begotten Son, that whoever believes in Him shall not perish, but have eternal life.* You will struggle with every aspect of being a G.R.O.W.N. Man without the help of Jesus Christ and all He wants you to do is accept Him as Lord in your life. The man you never knew will never become a reality unless you are willing to throw off the old man and put on the new man that a relationship with Christ provides, 2 *Corinthians 5:17 Therefore, if anyone is in Christ, he is a new creation; old things have passed away; behold, all things have become new.*

Will you accept Him? If you do then you will have really gained the true value of reading this book. Just as I have a hope for each of you to be navigated by your purpose; I believe part of my purpose was to write this book so that as a result of you reading this book you would either accept Jesus Christ in your life or strengthen your relationship with Him through prayer, reading His word, and being obedient to His word. I also realize that my purpose is connected to you. I am willing to be selfless and I am putting your needs before mine. You have a need for God, Jesus Christ, and the Holy Spirit in your life and I wrote this book for that very reason so that you could be in fellowship with them. We can together, me and you, fulfill God's purpose for our lives by taking the final step to Unlocking the G.R.O.W.N. Man within. Are you willing to become the man you never knew, well pray with me.

The G.R.O.W.N. Man's Prayer:

God I realized that I've been trying all types of things to become a man but I have failed time and time again. I now know that without you God I can never be the man that I was created to be. Father so forgive me of my sins, forgive me of everything that I've done in my life that pushed me farther and farther away from you. God, I am ready for the new life that is available to me through your son, Jesus Christ. Thank you for giving His life for me and thank you Jesus Christ for dying for my sins. Jesus I believe that you died for me and I want you to come into my life and be Lord over my life so that I can be in relationship with God, the Father, the one who holds the purpose for my life.

I submit my life to you now God, cause your Holy Spirit to come into my life and direct me. I don't have all the answers now but I know through your

Spirit I will be guided in the right direction. Grow me God into the G.R.O.W.N. Man that you have called me to be. God I realize that this is just the beginning and that now I must mature in you through prayer, reading your word, and being obedient to your word. Thank you for loving me and saving me, in Jesus name I pray, Amen!

1 Corinthians 13:11- " When I was a child, I spoke as a child, I understood as a child, I thought as a child; but when I became a man, I put away childish things."

MESSAGE TO THE
G.R.O.W.N. MEN

If you made the decision to accept Christ in your life or to strengthen your relationship with Christ; I am excited for what God has in store for you! Your journey towards becoming a G.R.O.W.N. Man is a rewarding journey but not always an easy journey.

If you made a committed decision to allow Jesus to be Lord over your life as a result of reading this book then there will be those that will try to stunt your growth and bring you back to the old man that you once were, but my hope for you is that you don't turn back. Remember don't rewrite the story that God has already written for you.

My advice for your new journey ahead is to begin reading a bible daily, begin praying daily, connect with others who have a relationship with Christ, and to begin attending church on a regular basis if at all possible. Don't get frustrated when things get difficult or if you mess up; God will grow you in your difficult times if you don't give up.

James 1:2-4, NASB Consider it all joy, my brethren, when you encounter various trials, ³ knowing that the testing of your faith produces endurance. ⁴ And let endurance have its perfect result, so that you may be perfect and complete, lacking in nothing.

I personally will be praying for you for the days ahead that your faith in God doesn't fail you. I love you with the love of Christ because we are now brothers in Christ! We are now connected because of your commitment to Christ and these are His words to you:

John 15:7-8, NIV ⁷ If you remain in me and my words remain in you, ask whatever you wish, and it will be done for you. ⁸ This is to my Father's glory, that you bear much fruit, showing yourselves to be my disciples.

Remain in Jesus my brother and all will be well! Jail cells, prison walls, or mental prisons can no longer confine you because Jesus has now set you free!

Sincerely Your Friend & Brother in Christ,

Keith

NOTES

1. "Character, Ethics, Morals and Values Defined." Character, Ethics, Morals and Values Defined. N.p., n.d. Web. 13 Feb. 2014.

2. Definition of Value in English:." Value: Definition of Value in Oxford Dictionary (American English) (US). N.p., n.d.

3. "The Sentencing Project Home." The Sentencing Project Home. N.p., n.d. Fri. 31 Jan. 2014.

www.ingramcontent.com/pod-product-compliance
Lightning Source LLC
Chambersburg PA
CBHW070546030426
42337CB00016B/2378